anythink

Pearl's New Tooth

A Book about Caring for Your Teeth

by Kerry Dinmont

Published by The Child's World®
1980 Lookout Drive • Mankato, MN 56003-1705
800-599-READ • www.childsworld.com

Photographs ©: Wave Break Media/Shutterstock Images, cover, 1, 3, 4, 10, 12; Shutterstock Images, 6, 14–15; iStockphoto, 9; Africa Studio/Shutterstock Images, 17; ESB Professional/Shutterstock Images, 18–19; Tinna Pong/ Shutterstock Images, 21

ISBN 9781503820227
LCCN 2016960947

Printed in the United States of America
PA02340

Pearl has a new tooth!

How does she care for her teeth?

Pearl uses floss once a day. She flosses in between her teeth.

Pearl brushes twice a day. She puts toothpaste on her brush. She uses just a bit of toothpaste.

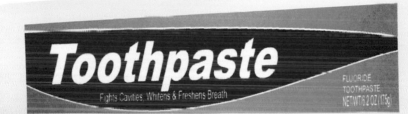

She brushes her teeth for two minutes. She is sure to brush every tooth.

Eating and drinking make teeth dirty. Brushing and flossing get rid of food and **germs**.

Pearl does not eat many sugary foods. Sugar is bad for teeth. It causes **cavities**.

Pearl goes to the dentist. The dentist will check for cavities.

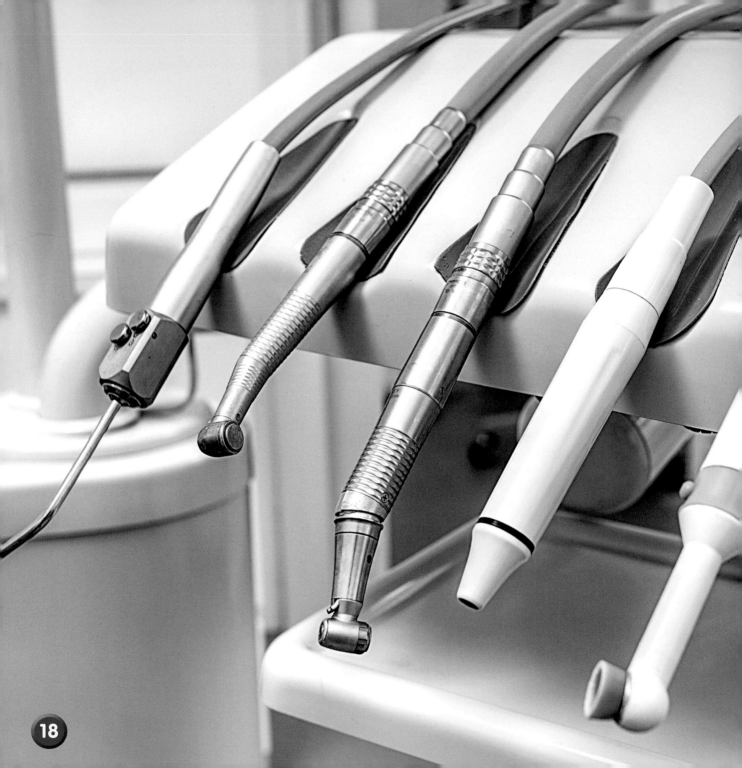

The dentist will use special tools to clean Pearl's teeth.

How do you care for
your teeth?

Glossary

cavities (KAV-i-teez) Cavities are holes in teeth. Sugar can wear away at teeth and form cavities.

germs (JURMZ) Germs are living things that are too small to see and cause disease. Pearl brushes her teeth to get rid of germs.

Extended Learning Activities

1. How do you take care of your teeth every day?

2. Have you gone to the dentist? What did your dentist tell you about your teeth?

3. Have you lost a tooth? Which tooth was it?

To Learn More

Books

Kawa, Katie. *My First Trip to the Dentist.*
New York, NY: Gareth Stevens Publishing, 2012.

Meister, Cari. *Dentists.* Minneapolis,
MN: Bullfrog Books, 2015.

Web Sites

Visit our Web site for links about teeth health:
childsworld.com/links

Note to Parents, Teachers, and Librarians: We routinely verify our Web links to make sure
they are safe and active sites. So encourage your readers to check them out!

About the Author

Kerry Dinmont is a children's book author who enjoys art and nature. She lives in Montana with her two Norwegian elkhounds.